Into the Dangerous World

Marina
WARNER

Into the Dangerous World

My mother groan'd, my father wept,
Into the dangerous world I leapt,
Helpless, naked, piping loud,
Like a fiend hid in a cloud . . .

William Blake, 'Infant Sorrow'

Chatto & Windus
LONDON

Published in 1989 by
Chatto & Windus Ltd
30 Bedford Square
London WC1B 3SG

A CIP catalogue record for this book
is available from the British Library

ISBN 0 7011 3548 4

Acknowledgements

Without the help of Sue Slipman, Director of the National Council for
One Parent Families, of Jo Roll, Family Policy Studies Centre and
Heather Joshi, Birkbeck College, London who gave advice and
information, and comments on the manuscript, I would not have been
able to write; to them, much gratitude.

My thanks to: all the participants and speakers at 'A Fairer Future?',
Child Poverty Action Group Conference, London, April, 1989 and at
'Children & Television – What's Going On?', BACTV Conference,
London, March, 1989. Also to Jenny Kuper, Rachel Hodgkin and
Nicola Wyld of the Children's Legal Centre; Valerie Yule, Faculty of
Education, Monash University, Australia; and Alexandra Artley,
London.

A full bibliography of the sources used is available on request.

Photoset in Linotron Ehrhardt by
Rowland Phototypesetting Ltd
Bury St Edmunds, Suffolk
Printed in Great Britain by
St Edmundsbury Press Limited, Bury St Edmunds, Suffolk

'The worst violence is poverty'

THERE ARE ten things wrong with this picture. See if you can spot them!

Oh yes, the cat is missing whiskers on the left side of its face. And the man working in the garden hasn't got a shoe on his right foot, the watering can's handle is missing, yes, and the dungarees of the toddler with him are held up by a miracle, as the fasteners have been left out . . .

(This is a game, from a Jumbo Book of Puzzles, to help pass the time.)

Here's another picture, there are some things wrong here too! See if you can spot them!

The bread-knife is lying on the floor . . . A packet of razor blades is on the table beside a bottle of pills with the cap off. Yes, there's a litre of bleach under the sink, and the door is open. A pan's bubbling on the gas stove and its handle is pointing over the edge . . . And the cat is about to spring on to the table and bring the cloth down with it . . . on top of the baby who is lying by the fire on the mat. There's no fireguard.

(This is another game, this is a game in a safety campaign poster pinned up in a hospital out-patient clinic to help pass the time waiting.)

* * *

But now this time it's a real room, and there are some things wrong here too!

(It isn't a game, not any more, this is a room in a bed & breakfast hotel, where someone lives with her children, where a family has been living for three years – in 'temporary accommodation'.)

But I'm not going to describe the things wrong in this picture – guilt-tripping is a last resource and besides, it's not the done thing today. It isn't necessary anyway in the case of children, there are other pleas to make. You've all seen the photographs in the newspapers and in the charity campaigns, and so you know. You don't need telling. Charities used to ask for money for children abroad, for wells in Africa and medicine in Asia. They still ask on their behalf, but they also beg for the have-nots here, and they can't meet the need.

The agencies who try and help look after the young who live in such rooms have a phrase for the problem. When the children haven't been 'abused', but there's something wrong just the same, they call it: 'failure to thrive'. This is what happens to people in rooms like the one in the picture: they fail to thrive. This is what is happening to children here: they are failing to thrive.

Around seven million people in Britain have only known this government and its prime minister all their lives, because they were small in 1979 or born since. They are Thatcher's children. This is a plural society, as we all know, and needless to say, the factors that make up pluralism aren't equal. When the Secretary of State for Social Security replied to the

2

question put to him at the end of last year by Frank Field, MP, How many people are living on Income Support? the minister answered, for the government, 4,354,000.

(There were 2,855,000 on Supplementary Benefit in the year the Conservatives put the economy back on the road, in 1979 – almost half the number.)

These four million odd claimants have 3,018,000 partners and children. (In 1979, the figure for dependents of those on SB was one and a half million.) Of those three million odd 'dependents', 2,111,000 are under sixteen years old.

Income Support is the new name for SB, a part of the new benefit system, with Family Credit and the Social Fund. The system provides variable sums, rising and falling in relation to dependents and other factors, but they never amount to very much – they mean the bottom of the heap in our prosperous country; they provide a useful measure of what John Moore prefers to call 'inequality', not poverty, maintaining the differentials in a manner that's only just, getting around a problem that used to loom – working people getting less than loafers. These benefits are targeted, and are meant to cut down the overall state bill for family support by reaching only those families in need. Like Reagan's administration, this government is committed to giving money away on a strictly means-tested basis. This sounds fine, and, to well-off mothers feeling guilty about their right to universal Child Benefit, it even sounds just; but the dramatic rise in family poverty in the United States since closely focused means-tested benefits came in should clarify our comparable slide down into squalor and negligence. Take-up has been poor, just as in America – people are abashed about coming forward to be assessed, they do not have time to make the approaches, they are worried about loans from the Social Fund, which usually have to be repaid, they fear other strings attached – like supervision, or the disapproval of employers. This government has represented benefits as somehow shameful. The point about *universal* benefits is that they affirm the value of such social tasks as having children, rearing them, or caring for relatives; they make benefits themselves an expression of collective approval for the endeavour, not begrudged hand-outs, stigmatising the recipients as beggars and failures.

In response to the reluctant take-up of the new benefits, the government has bought television time and the sides of London buses to spread the good news about Family Credit's accessibility: glum paragons encourage you to come forward, to discover that you too can dig into the bran tub. It's an attempt to put a good face on the situation, but it must be an irony that some previously universal benefits (the Maternity Grant) have been stopped and others frozen (Child Benefit) and that now money is being spent coaxing people to come and get sums they might have got automatically in the first place.

The Prime Minister and her colleagues are the apostles of self-reliance; yet the freezing of universal Child Benefit (£7.25 a week for each child) this year for the second time has meant that the mothers of 60,000 more children have been pushed into the

4

claimants lists. The introduction of selective principles brutally underlines differences between families, when childhood should be a time of equality, of possibility, if not background circumstances.

The definition of poverty varies from one vantage-point or another, and the benefit figures do not give a clear or full picture. When an institution, like the National Foster Care Association, tries to arrive at the cost of a child, it produces a scale of differing rates for babies, children and teenagers. But in all cases the sums it recommends be given to families undertaking this work are over twice as much as the state benefits reckon. After means-testing, this government stays mean. Hating dependents, this government has doubled their number; and has still not met the need.

Figures are boring, numbers break your head, they're never up to date: the ruler doesn't measure the same inch and the statisticians always have the latest figures to change the picture. But not this picture. Whichever way you take it – with irritation that so many are still living off the nanny state, with stricken conscience, or with fellow feeling – the multitude of the poor speaks of a failure of government, of a tragic deterioration over the decade in the condition of childhood.

The changes have produced new tensions and perils for all children. Don't listen when people murmur about the old days, about chimney-sweeps and going down the mines and how children have never had it so good. Forget Beethoven's mother's syphilis and Charlie Chaplin in the Lambeth workhouse. Geniuses might rise from the slums, but society's duty doesn't lie with producing geniuses first. Comparisons with the past are of limited help: the ending of hanging won't make the suicides in youth remand centres go away; the mortality, famine, rickets, scabies of Victorian slum children don't turn free school milk into an excessive luxury. John Moore – and his family – would wither if they had to live in the conditions he denies exist. The Eastenders whom Maud Pember Reeves described in her pioneering *Round About a Pound a Week* had different expenses, but a telly isn't an extravagance in a family today, no more than a washing machine. Yet the mother of a two-week-old baby was recently sent to prison – for not paying her TV licence.

The changes in the character of childhood aren't however confined among the horrifying thousands of children in penury. They can be discerned among the prosperous too, because the condition of one child touches that of another, is part of the main. Impoverishment can be an intangible too, but it cries less loudly for help than the tangible sort – and it is harder to reverse. When goods become the highest good, children cannot be expected to hold out, on their own, for a different morality. Inequality is catching. Children inherit principles; they do not set them.

It's a truism that poverty in Britain would be riches in Ethiopia; but our society is wealthy. And in a society like ours, the first, most urgent question is, With the means and resources we have, what can we do? And then, let's not stop there, let's also put the question, Besides what is possible and hasn't been done, what should be done? '"Suggest what is practicable" people keep saying to me,' Rousseau wrote in *Emile*. 'It's as if you told me, "Suggest doing what is being done, or at least, suggest some good which combines with the existing evil."'

In November this year the United Nations Convention on the rights of the child is likely to be adopted; it declares 'the right of every child to a standard of living adequate for the child's physical, mental, spiritual, moral and social development.'

Will Britain sign it?

Could Britain sign it?

In good faith?

Hamburger and French Fries

For children, McDonald's is a treat. They ask to go to McDonald's for their birthdays. On Saturdays, they're thick on the ground, with their Saturday fathers. They like the eating methods required, the opening and the munching and the sucking and the dipping and the crumpling and the tossing; they love the taste of the grease.

One weekday, after school, a mother is standing by the door to my local McDonald's with a baby. They're pointing up the street, away from the hamburgers and fries, but she's come to a halt and her head is turned to her other child, who has the glass door open. She is listening to him, with a kind of patience that's known as maternal, but which is the expression underdogs learn in order to avoid getting hit.

This is passive resistance. The child hanging on the door is around eight. He is shouting:

'Give me the money!'

When his order does not move her, when he sees it slip off her like the rain on the buggy's plastic, he becomes frenzied, he grips the door and levitates with rage.

'GIVE ME THE MONEY!'

She turns, she makes her way up the street. But she doesn't rebuke him. It's almost as if, in the midst of her refusal, she recognises his behaviour as normal.

There's a poster in the window. McDonald's is offering a prize for a Child of Achievement. You can nominate anyone you know, a violinist, a swimmer, a computer wiz. You don't even have to send in coupons proving you've eaten the ten millionth chicken nugget or the six billionth Big Mac. McDonald's has the interests of children at heart.

A rosier picture

SOME improvements have taken place: the eighties have seen the value of children recognised in unprecedented ways for Britain; the concept of childhood has been redefined to emphasise or increase its prerogatives and importance. Children, representing the future of society, have come to symbolise the potential for good, personal and social, and their recognition as persons has been accompanied by a new emphasis on individuality.

Bastardy has at last disappeared from the lawbooks: the sins of the fathers (and the mothers) are no longer to be visited on the children. The phrase 'child abuse' has entered public consciousness, not because the acts it describes did not exist before, but because they were overlooked, as children counted for less than the grown-ups in charge of them. The struggles to right these and other wrongs have led to radical reforms which have altered the status in law of the child. The Cleveland crisis, the failed attempts of Victoria Gillick to consolidate parental authority over teenagers, and the new Children's Bill have led to new, unexpectedly far-reaching rights for children, and curbed the licence of adults over them. 'A child is a person, not an object of concern', said Justice Butler-Sloss in her report on the Cleveland cases of child abuse. She directed those in contact with young people – doctors,

9

police, social workers, teachers, as well as parents – to pay attention to what they had to say, and to let them speak. Family Courts have not been included in the Children's Bill, as yet, but there are strong hopes they may come, and with them, increased consultation with all parties, and a diminishment of lawyers' powers to exploit injuries. In the country where 'Children should be seen and not heard' was a shibboleth, where 'Find out what the children are doing and tell them not to' was the rule of thumb, children are now to be heeded; in this way at least, we are living in child-centred times.

The fundamental but subtle shift in priorities has found its voice in the law as a more important principle: after Mrs Gillick lost her case in the House of Lords, Lord Denning said, 'Parental powers are not bestowed on parents in recognition of the important role they play in society or as recompense for their efforts in caring for your children. Powers must be exercised for the benefit of the child, and if challenged must be justified in terms of the child's protection and welfare.'

The child comes first. The judge's words clarified a position that many reformers and compassionate movements had striven for since Lord Shaftesbury and Dr Barnardo. Parents do not own their children to do with them what they will; the authority of the father has shrunk and shrunk since the 1840s; while the authority of the mother had never enjoyed such a long rule in law, in spite of the sacredness of the maternal vocation and other received ideas. Until the law of 1973 (yes, only sixteen years ago) established equal parental rights, mothers could forfeit their children for much less reason than fathers; custody of their offspring, and their authority over them, were never enshrined as securely as paternal power: in divorce cases before 1873, an adulterous husband could keep the children, but an adulterous wife had to give them up. Victoria Gillick, struggling to establish maternal control according to her own lights, incidentally helped to define a new autonomy for children. A child is no longer the chattel of either parents or guardians, and cannot be used or directed solely as they think fit.

The resolution of the Gillick case wasn't altogether revolutionary, for, as Lord Denning said, the law only follows a lead society sets; it cannot fly in the face of common belief and practice. To deem infant buggery against natural justice does not seem surprising; and to move from the consideration of that crime to limiting the prerogatives of parents does not seem a big step. Yet not very long ago, it would have been unheard of to pry into family life and prevent such horror, especially if the perpetrator were the father, and many of the parents in the Cleveland crisis as well as the media on their behalf were indignant on the grounds of family sanctity and privacy. The social worker figured as a witchhunter, the tool of the state's interference; the doctors as diabolical inquisitors. (Salem was invoked by the local MP.)

Lord Denning's words sum up a fundamental change with far-reaching implications because they characterise parenthood as trusteeship, not ownership. The separate status of children, vis-à-vis adults in charge of them, had never been given so much consideration before. Nor was the value of children reckoned so very dear. The National Society for the Protection of Children was after all founded in Liverpool in 1884, *after* the RSPCA. Britain still has a high rate of infant death, higher than most other European countries, and it used to be worse.

Britain was also the last developed country where beating schoolchildren was respectable. This was outlawed last year – by one vote in parliament. Parents are now almost the last people left who can hit their own children without fear of penalty, as long as it's moderate and fitting punishment. There's some talk, in the wake of the Children's Bill, of trying to outlaw parents hitting children too, as in Sweden. Smacking an offence? The idea makes people giggle at best, sneer at worst; others fear it would drive punishment behind doors. But changes in the law can lead shifts in sensibility and judgement: setting aside questions of justice and dignity, a hug can be more efficient discipline than a blow. But the language of authority still derives from violence, mistakenly, tragically.

The ages of childhood

PEOPLE ARE children for longer than they used to be, and in the West for longer than in other parts of the world. In Britain, childhood is elastic. It lasts a very long time if you want to claim Income Support – if unmarried or childless, you have to be twenty-five to qualify for the adult rate; before that, you are still assumed to be dependent on your parents and can only receive a reduced sum. (These are changes since the old Supplementary Benefit.) But if you have crime in mind, you are deemed separable from your family rather earlier (you can be prosecuted at the age of eight in Scotland or ten in England). If you want to earn money through work, it's against the law before the age of thirteen, though many under-age children reported to the Exeter University annual survey that they held a variety of jobs, with the familiar newspaper round leading the way. It was compulsory to stay at school until the age of ten at the end of the last century, although many ignored this restriction. The age limit gradually rose through the first decades of this century, until 1973, when the present minimum school-leaving age of sixteen was established. At this stage several other things become lawful, all demarcating a change from childhood to adulthood: sex (for girls – boys are different, are allowed to do it younger), a passport, marriage, fireworks, not to mention smoking, drinking, and tattoos. The vote, as we know, comes at eighteen, as does the nowadays equally heavy responsibility of a credit card.

In Britain, independence doesn't always follow children attaining their majority. No shared ritual marks the end of parents' responsibility; autonomy has to be negotiated in every individual child's case. The Thatcher years have seen a sustained prolonging of childhood, as a consequence of the government commitment to the family and parental responsibility. It is much tougher financially for children to leave home, because of reforms to the benefit structure and the obligations of the Youth Training Scheme, and while eighteen-year-olds aren't treated as full adults when benefits are at stake, they will be when it comes to the Poll Tax – unless they're studying full-time.

Tightening the links between teenagers and their families has paradoxically swelled the numbers of runaways: since money is one of the chief causes of family quarrels, the increased, stage-managed dependence of youth on the Training Scheme can make life at home an intolerable strain, for parents and offspring alike. At the same time, since Britain endures one of the shabbiest records in Europe for higher education, and students from poorer families are declining in numbers, there's a bigger crowd of unskilled teenagers living at home to cope with. Fewer students, fewer sixth formers, fewer passes at the equivalent of 'A' level, fewer teachers, than in France for instance; and what of the children who haven't yet gone to school, what of them? As the T-shirt says, the future isn't what it used to be.

A cigarette

It is the week before Christmas, a pleasant night in the winter
of 1988, the winter that was unusually warm. I have been to
the Tennessee Williams play, Orpheus Descending; it is a
melodrama, about the redemptive power of sexual love. I am
with friends, and it's late when we finish eating, the last tube
has gone, but we aren't in a hurry, we are enjoying what
begins to feel like an escapade in a foreign city. Chauffeurs
are smoking outside gambling clubs with Christmas trees in
every glowing window, and waiters are strong-arming giant
dustbins into the alleys where the vagrants are waiting to pick
them over. After a while, and no taxis, we begin to wonder
how we'll get home. We reach the Hilton, where there's a
long queue. Youths in dj's are propping up girls in ballooning
taffeta, drooping off the shoulder; the night is filled with late
mating calls. I am staring. My eye hovers, passes, goes back.
He sees me looking at him. He's sharply dressed, in a silky
Italian woven jacket with notable buttons (not quite the nauti-
cal nostalgia of Visconti's Tadzio, but the bell sounds); he's
drawing on a cigarette with a perfected nonchalance. I recognise that way of smoking, I did it like that when I was
young. Defiance is needed to meet the tobacco's surprising
strength. I can't help staring, though our exchange of glances
is fleeting, and he says to me, with his eyes, not, What the
fuck are you staring at? (which is what a gipsy child smoking
in the tube at Camden Town once spat at me) but 'Don't you
dare.' He was about thirteen, I suppose, and he was working
his patch, right outside the Hilton Hotel, just to the side of
the revolving doors, not quite in the crowd queuing for taxis,
but near enough to melt into it if anyone decided to accost
him for the wrong reason.

The Privatised Child

'There is no such thing as society. There are individual men and women and there are families.'

Mrs Thatcher, 1989

ON THE WHOLE, children lose value as they grow, while they also begin to cost more. The younger the child, the more precious he or she is; for some the unborn child is sacred to a degree the teenager never attains. The reluctant baby of dreams is sought after in infertility clinics by an ever increasing number of couples (around 30,000 in 1986 – with 605 successful in vitro inseminations that year). Youth itself is treasured, and when it is cut short – when, for instance the number of teenage mothers rises, as it did in the sixties – the reaction on the whole is anxiety and compassion on the mothers' behalf, for missing out on their childhood.

There's no longer so much need for distress over this. Young people are no longer having babies the way they used to. Though the numbers of single mothers have risen overall, the proportion of them under twenty years old has fallen: the majority are now older, and are divorced or separated. The average age of a mother in Britain at the birth of her first child is now twenty-six; the rate of birth tapered in the late seventies, then rose very slightly and has remained steady, not only among teenagers but in all groups, though some professional women are managing to have a first baby in the nick of time, putting the birthrate for forty-year-old mothers at an unusual high. More and more people are only having one child, too. We are not replacing ourselves. There were many more young people at the beginning of the eighties than there will be at the beginning of the nineties. Old people will outnumber them, maybe even by two to one, and so the young will have to graft to produce the wealth to pay the pledged pensions – maybe this is why David Willetts, the director of the Centre of Policy Studies and a Thatcher adviser, said recently, 'I would like to see a return to the values that made children feel that their elderly parents were first and foremost their responsibility, not the state's.' Maybe the birthrate will start going up if parents realise their future prosperity may depend on it – but will their children want to maintain the older generation? Will they in turn be able to afford to have children themselves if their parents take the place of offspring as dependents?

Demographic projections have their faults, and societies, fortunately, are volatile and even capable of taking a turn for the better. But when you look at these population figures for Britain, they show one or two things that skew the sweet-talk about the ideal self-reliant and close-knit family we have been hearing so much about over the last ten years. A lot of people aren't having children because they anticipate the expense. Some Dinkies – Dual Income No Kids – value their disposable incomes more than a possible family; others are so heavily mortgaged they recall the seventeenth century aristocrats who were landpoor, possessing lots of acres but no cash. Property prices and mortgage rates have bloated in accord with the combined earning power of a husband and wife working full-time, so some new professional couples, even if they don't want to, have to remain Dinkies to meet their monthly payments.

If you can afford shares in a family, you can go ahead and buy. Like gas and water and other aspects of existence that used to seem solid and dependable, even essential, securities, to which citizens had an unquestioned right of access, children have been turned into high-risk acquisitions. The child of the eighties has been privatised too. A lot of people who have children have too much tied up in them, and can't make ends meet; and, like failing companies, the government views their collapse without mercy: 1,100 children with a single parent were taken into care last year because they were homeless. Simple, you would think, to prevent this, to house a child and its mother. But no, it looks now as if the right to a home will be taken away from a woman who is expecting a baby, if she's single: these kind of babies should be discouraged, they're different, it seems, from babies born to married women. They're less welcome. Though this mother too becomes a stockholder in the national firm, her dividends aren't to be paid. There's a gradual move taking place towards a carrot-and-stick style of support, rewarding certain behaviour, punishing others. John Redwood, MP, recently suggested that unmarried mothers should be placed in hardship housing – *pour encourager les autres*. Such an attitude looks suspiciously like a spur to terminating pregnancies; since these mothers could have chosen not to have a child. Curious, when the party of the family finds itself by implication the party of abortion.

There is a yet deeper conflict at the core of the Conservatives' attitude to the family: between the privatisation of the child financially and the liberation of the child legally. The clash is making things worse for children, empowering them as individuals distinct from their parents, when they are economically at their parents' mercy. It is making things worse for parents, too, for they feel vulnerable to punishment from their children if they fail them or appear to fail them; and poverty (sorry, inequality) has come to seem one of the ways a family fails its members, just as it has come to seem the way citizens fail their society, and not society its citizens.

On the one hand, John Patten (Minister at the Home Office and the chairman of the Ministerial Group on Women's Issues) wants to batten down the nuclear family into an indivisible entity, moving, thinking, being as one, so that the parents become responsible for the behaviour of the children to such a degree that they take the rap for their offences. On the other hand, the market force child requires food and shelter according to the law of the market, and parents must work to provide them. The Out of School Alliance, a body campaigning for childcare, reckons that a fifth of all children between the ages of five and ten are left alone at home after school, and even more in the holidays; as the only child is more and more common, these 'latch-key' children are truly left on their own. Britain has a dismal record for supervised sports grounds, or safe play spaces – cars (and the way they're driven) have made the streets unsafe for city children, the popular beaches are filthy, the sea polluted with sewage and other poisons. As the director of the NSPCC, Alan Gilmour, has observed, 'Better training of parents and professionals, and above all, better routine surveillance of young children are essential, if thousands of lives are not to be blighted every year.'

Nappies

The babies are bare-bottomed on their mothers' arms in Quattrocento paintings; in the nineteenth century, boys, as well as girls, wore frocks until they were trained so that their nappies could be changed more easily. Eskimos used sphagnum moss, naturally soft, naturally absorbent. Nearer home, nappies used to be made of rags, torn into strips and washed over and over – tough work. Then the washing machine was invented, and Britain led the world in terry towelling, and the Harrington Square, most prestigious of brands. The disposable pads that came in in the sixties changed women's lives again – no more smell of pee and disinfectant from the nappy bucket lingering in the home. Instead, a pad could be laid inside a plastic sheet and tied onto the baby; the plastic, once wet, made weals on their skin; soon that was solved by the fully fashioned Pampers brand (I first saw these in America, when they hadn't yet crossed the Atlantic, and they struck me as miraculous). Now the Friends of the Earth say the bleach used to whiten the pulp nappies are made of contains dioxin which is poisonous – to the baby, as well as to the food chain. Disposable nappies are also expensive, theoretically less expensive than running a washing machine at the high temperatures and for the length of time needed to clean a nappy, but still, expensive.

In Boots' one morning, by the Baby Counter, a young man, his baby in a stroller under the plastic canopy, was bobbing around his wife on springy heels. He is saying, 'You tell me, we need it all, so, we need it.'

She looks at him mildly, with an indulgent pleasure, as if hearing him talk at all is doing her good. She is almost giggling at the fuss he's making.

He jabs at her, but pulls away from touching her, just at the last moment. She never flinches, just reads the label on a jar of baby food.

'What d'you think of this, then?' she asks him.

'She needs that too, does she?' He pokes with a trainer-covered foot at the invisible child under the plastic canopy of the buggy. 'She has to have that as well, does she?'

His partner still has a sort of blissed-out look as she listens to him, and nods.

They make their way to the till; the young father is hopping on his fat-soled shoes. As they leave, the mother pushes the stroller, with its new burden of nappies and other baby products, through the swing doors, which he holds for them, looking as if he knows he has to. In the street outside, he bends down and shouts through the plastic at the child,

'You cost six pounds thirty-seven, you did.' Then again, louder; there's no response from inside. 'Six pounds thirty-seven.'

Mothers at Work

MOST MARRIED women with school-age children work part-time only; the responsibility they assume often costs them the securities of regular work, the pensions and sick leave and possibility of advancement, not to mention the higher pay, or the better quarters which an income would make possible. The amount a father would have to pay to provide for his child without a mother varies tremendously – some full-time help (a nanny) costs rather more than other ad hoc child-minding; one survey in 1987, by Legal and General, reckoned a wife's work would cost £370 a week. The married state brings the man advantages in his job, too: family men appear to have better prospects, whereas family women (doesn't the phrase sound pleonastic?) are often passed over in favour of unattached and childless female colleagues. The cost of a child to a working woman over her lifetime is hard to calculate – but Heather Joshi, an economist at Birkbeck College, University of London, has put the figure for a mother with two children at around £135,000 over a working life, by reckoning missed career prospects and pensions with the actual expenses of child-rearing. All women – married, unmarried, in work, out of work – keep house more than men, shouldering the 'double burden'; many men do not share the family income with the woman, so that it is her earnings which often pay for the children's needs and day-to-day household costs. This is why Child Benefit should go on being paid to the mother.

One of the most significant changes in British life in the last ten years has been the rise in single mothers: families headed by one parent alone have increased over the decade by nearly a quarter, to over a million households at the last estimate. A surprising number of widows (and some widowers) are still represented – they used to form a far greater proportion, before the seventies. Unmarried mothers now make up about a fifth of the total, and the trend has been rising, partly because few give away children for adoption. About half of the babies born outside marriage are registered by the mother and father together, suggesting that they live in common law marriages, post-sixties re-lationships which may seek to escape the jinx of official unions by pledging love privately. (These babies do not figure among the numbers of single parent families on Income Support: their mothers count as married.) The largest number of single parents are divorced or separated (no one uses the word 'deserted' any more; and of course, not all of them are 'deserted'). One in seven families with children has a woman alone as the head of the household; the number of children living with a divorced mother has trebled since the seventies (to around 1.6 million), and it is forecast that by the age of sixteen, one in five children will have experienced divorce if the present curve continues.

It might be expected that single parents would also work part-time, like married women, because after all, they are even more needed at home. Yet more of these single parents – most of whom are women – work full-time rather than part-time. They do this in the face of social disapproval, too, for 'most people still feel' – three quarters of the sample in the Exeter University report – that women with small children should stay at home. This number has been shrinking over the years, however, in keeping with dramatically increased support for mothers working when the children are older. More single mothers also work full-time rather than part-time because the poverty trap opens when earnings are small – reducing benefits, and increasing tax – thus producing the very effect the government fears, that many single mothers are discouraged from working at all.

You have to be rich to be a child whose mother stays at home; or, you have to accept to be poor. The income of women on their own with a child or children stands at under half the income of couples; and is falling. The maintenance payment ordered by the court is rarely paid (there aren't any figures for defaulters, but a fraction – only six per cent – of women rely completely on maintenance). New guidelines to government departments now allow a child to search records to find his or her missing parent; the normal confidentiality can be waived. This provision could help women trace the shirkers too. However, far from being alimony parasites and idlers, very few divorced women live off their former husbands, even when they have had children. The wife 'who takes him to the cleaner's', who makes a career of divorce, is rare, and usually well-off in the first place (enough to afford lawyers); she – and the media who feed on her spite – do the thousands of hard-working poverty-stricken women an immense injustice, which the courts should not allow. Most women prefer not to have to deal with their former partner any more, and it is degrading and distressing – as well as wasteful of valuable time that could be spent earning or caring for home and family – to put the law on someone.

That so many women on their own keep their families is a reality that the government will not face. Remedies have been suggested, mainly by the EEC, as Britain is not the only country to be experiencing these changes: more rights for part-time workers, job sharing, training schemes for returners, but above all, where children are concerned, childcare.

The stubborn loyalty of the Thatcherite Tories to privately funded services makes Britain the only country to refuse the EEC directives on the provision of crêches, kindergartens and parental leave. The family doctrines of the Romantics among the Tories, who want Mum to stay at home with the sparkling laundry, are suffering defeat at the hands of the Pragmatists, who look at the job market in the next few decades and realise that more Mums are going to have to go out to work even more than they are already, and that something will have to be done about the children. From a monetarist point of view, the people supply is running out, and sweet dreams about family life must end in theory, as well as in practice. The government has realised that if there are to be enough children, future workers making enough money to support the ageing population, the fragrant woman of

Tory dreams is going to work – full-time, not just part-time, on proper lifelong careers (like breadwinners, like men). If she is to have children at all, something will have to be done to encourage her, to help her look after them. But the government sets its face against any giving help from the state. The Prime Minister replied to Linda Kelsey of *Cosmopolitan* at the meeting of the Society of Women's Magazine Editors: 'If women wish to go out to work, they can afford childcare. Otherwise employers can take care of it.'

Facing the spectre of the falling work-force, some institutions have reacted: the Midland Bank has started a career break scheme which allows women to leave to have their babies and then return to the same job; it is also planning to start crêches and nurseries in the banks for its employees. But in matters that help families care for their offspring, like leave for both parents at the birth of a child or during illness, state nurseries, schools for under-fives, places where children can play safely and interestingly after school hours and during the holidays, tax allowances for child expenses, Britain lags behind countries like France or even Italy, thought to be atavistically attached to homebound Mamma and paternal authority.

It's women's luck, perhaps, that as needed workers they play a part in those market forces and can help to shape them. The successful professionals can make demands: if the firm can offer a company car, it can afford a childcare allowance. The trade unions, in collaboration with some big employers, are also working out conditions for mothers. Only large firms will be able to afford such measures, of course, and then they will probably treat them as perks rather than as rights. Nurseries in the place of work mean that small children have to join the commuters' rush hours; nor will they be with local friends from different strands in society, but only with the children of their parents' workmates and colleagues. As for parents working in small firms, they will still have to cast about to find a minder whose wage is small enough to make their own wages worth the getting; the government, in its passion for deregulation and its aversion to local authorities, at first made no stipulations about qualifications for the task of childminding, no conditions, and no direction, until the risks of such a happy-go-lucky approach were pointed out, and amendments to the Children's Bill introduced.

Childcare for working parents does not only mean daytime care for infants, but improved conditions in the schools. Education itself is beyond the scope of this pamphlet, but the question of nourishment isn't. When Mrs Thatcher's first action as a minister was to stop free school milk ('Thatcher, Thatcher, Milk Snatcher'), she well and truly showed her hand, then and there. One of the early steps the government took was to drop national standards of nutrition as well. Previously, schools offered a hot meal to everyone, and were obliged to apportion so much protein, so many vitamins to children; now, they do fast food and free school meals have become more and more restricted. The market was henceforward to determine which children would be decently nourished, and from the womb onwards: the new cuts in family

28

benefits now impoverish the diet of future mothers too.

Army inspectors during the conscription of World War One were startled by the numbers of young men they had to turn away because they were suffering from malnutrition. It was chronic in Britain in the years of Edwardian plenty, just as it is returning now in the affluence of the eighties among the children who live on crisps and cake and ketchup. The lowest fifth of the population spend a larger proportion of their income on food than the wealthy – because they don't buy other things, of course. But children are also softer targets for the huge industry of prepared and fast food, in which so many prosperous people have a stake. Those who look after children – so often the mother – haven't got the stamina to fight kids with food that isn't like the brand product steaming on the telly, or haven't the means to cook at home anyway. Working mothers spend a quarter as much again on food as women who don't work; and in the B & B hotels among the homeless, there are only single gas-rings or shared kitchenettes. New words for eating – 'snacking' and 'grazing' – have entered English, to express the habits children have formed. When a child in a rich country is sickly because of the quality of the food he or she is eating, then society is committing a criminal injustice. As the journalist Alexandra Artley comments, 'the National Health service was set up as the curative side of a whole health programme, in which free school meals figured as part of the preventive medicine that is also necessary for the health of children and society.' When John Patten proposed that parents should be considered responsible for the crimes of their offspring, the National Association of Probation Officers commented that it would be better to provide decent housing and food and school facilities before punishing the parents.

So often, penalties take precedence over prevention, retribution displaces provision. The government is proud of its prison building – twenty-six new ones between 1983 and 1995 to house the growing population of prisoners; equally, they are justly proud that, for the first time, children will be encouraged to give evidence of their own wishes in contested divorces, according to the Children's Bill. Of course, if there are to be more crimes, it is best to help the perpetrators to reform, and not shut them up in a hell-hole to train them that dog eats dog. Of course, if there are to be broken marriages, by all means, let's hear it from the children. I suppose we should be glad that somewhere like Manchester free meals were still being supplied to over half the school population in 1987. But the reason may make one pause. The children qualified on a means test, in spite of new restrictions: their parents or parent did not have enough money to feed them themselves. Moreover, when the new conditions were introduced in April 1988, 7000 children in that city had to start to pay or bring in a lunch box with cold food. The new benefit reforms also rule that local authorities can no longer give meals at their own discretion: the child who does not bring lunch to school but is not poor enough to qualify will not eat at all.

Some of the reforms needed to rescue the situation

of children are so entangled in other matters that they are hard to propose, let alone execute. But daily bread for school-children? Again, should children be allowed to suffer from neglect because of some theory about the family's sole responsibility?

Improvements to the conditions of working women will not sap the foundations of family life; rather, they are likely to strengthen them. Marriage is not failing, not here: it's still more popular in the UK than any other country in the EEC. To raise the quality of a mother's life can only make life better for the children, and to help children is to accept a civilised responsibility for the future, in the face of the last ten years' *immediatismo*, the new Tory avidity, the focus on the present, the quick turnover, and instant profits. And to help the children of the family when there's no such thing as society but only families, would appear a matter of urgency, no?

A Father

Some fathers are full-time, but most are Saturday fathers. Some Saturday fathers are Sunday fathers, too; but in general on Sundays, most become part of Sunday families. Some would like to be fathers on other days, but they go to work at jobs which require their undivided attention. It's difficult for a man to say he's staying home because one of the children has been up all night with colic. Mothers can call in with reason – that's why so many women's jobs aren't so important, nor so well paid, and come without pensions or perks or other recognitions of value. So many women are *replaceable*. You see fathers on Saturdays, wandering around. They tend not to use pushchairs. When they carry infants in pouches, they can sometimes look awkward, as if they're in fancy dress and the shoes pinch. Or they brandish their competence: even if the male chest doesn't fit, even if it doesn't have the right hollows, they still know how to cradle an infant.

Weekday fathers – you see them in the supermarket, with the whole family, ticking off items on the budget, balancing the sums – usually seem more physically at ease with little ones. It's one benefit of being home all day unemployed, that you get to know your children when they're awake.

Some Saturday fathers want to make sure they aren't branded by domesticity. In the fish shop, a youth in cowboy boots and a buzz haircut has a three-year-old girl in tow. He asks for some fish.

'What would you like?' replies the fishmonger, politely, surveying the display.

'Haven't a clue!' says the young Saturday father, casually.

'She never said, did she, doll?' He bends over his little girl, adjusts her jeans jacket. 'You decide!' he tells the fishmonger, pleasantly.

Another Saturday father, who works mornings (he's a milkman), takes the nipper on the float with him. With pleasure, they ride together, and the boy rings the front door bells and fetches the money to his dad. 'How he's grown,' the customers cluck. The Saturday father can step out in pride; he walks abroad, he goes to the park, he makes the world visible to his child: 'Here are some ducks, here is an oak tree, this is an old lady, is she a witch? I don't think so, do you? I hope the world will be good to you.' He is happy, now that his fear of coping with the tiny and fragile form has been overcome. He thinks mothers don't have such a hard time, really. He wonders whether he would like to be mother instead.

In the name of the fathers

'A mother's place is in the wrong.'

Dr Wendy Greengross

THE ROLE of father has received more attention in recent years than the husband's: its duties and obligations, its rewards and its strains are widely circulated, and some passionate testimonials have been written, like Ian McEwan's thoughtful *A Child in Time*. Tradition still articulates a woman's tasks in a marriage, royal and presidential glamour – Nancy Reagan, Princess Di – reinforce the Puritan ideal of the wife as helpmeet, as the necessary support of her husband, as well as his total dependent, holding up as model a kind of marriage that is economically impossible for most members of the population, entailing long absences from home, no earnings by the woman, and a couture wardrobe. But the duties of a husband are not even discussed; the character of the role is buried in assumptions about natural relations and social norms, and these are radically changing, without any scrutiny. Emotionally, financially, socially, what does a man owe the woman with whom he lives, to whom he is married?

One of the ironic effects of calls for women's independence has been the withdrawal of men as protectors in a world that has put almost nothing else in their place, and has not provided women with many means to help themselves. At the beginning of the decade, I believed that women were on their way to self-sufficiency, that they could not ask for equality and special provisions at the same time. Now I have come to realise that unless opportunities are given, from birth onwards, to girls and their mothers in the form of positive rights, unless the social and material dependency of women on men weakens, and the responsibilities of boys and their fathers are properly considered, the effects of the changes in relations between the sexes will contribute to children's distress. A philosophy of marriage as an alliance needs urgently to be developed and circulated; an alliance in which the parties are equal, with interests and needs that should be equally served. Meanwhile, a lot of the time (I know it's not all the time), it's the men what get the pleasure, and the wives what get the blame.

After the break-up of a marriage, many fathers no longer visit their children at all after the first six months. They lose interest, disappear altogether. More divorced men remarry than divorced women, and acquire new interests in another family. There are more mothers than fathers in Britain, and more lone mothers and fewer lone fathers than there were; a lot of men marry twice, and some produce new families to look after.

If a woman abandons her children, some people might understand, but they do not condone it; few people however think badly of the father who leaves one family for another. It is the way things are. As the economist Heather Joshi commented, 'One of the many advantages of being male is that it is easier to opt out of the obligation to maintain than it is to opt out of the unwritten obligation to care.'

The sanctification of family holds out a promise of ceaseless narcissistic gratification; motherhood, especially, is exalted in the abstract for its fulfilment and satisfactions. But when, in practice, the woman lives with 'motherism', with gynephobia and prejudice, when the pleasures of having a child are complicated by disappointments and stresses, expectations of fulfilment are dealt a deep wound which can endanger family relations. Whereas a pregnant woman will inspire help from strangers, she'll soon find, when the baby becomes a toddler, that people will avoid her, from the moment when the baby starts to throw things on the ground, or cries, or won't sit still. (Though sometimes, in my experience, the mother's fear of causing trouble exceeds others' impatience and disapproval.) Maternal instincts are assumed to be constant against all trials, mothering an inborn, untaught capacity that any woman can do anywhere; consequently, there has been no review of maternity, one of the most crucial social tasks, since 1948.

Because the occupation of mother still establishes a woman – however vaguely – as a useful citizen, because women are given credit for knowing how to do this job at least better than men, motherhood becomes a desired locus of female power, almost the only locus to which young women have access, as Beatrix Campbell described in her study of Wigan Pier fifty years after Orwell. But it also places the new mother in a state of neediness, or reliance on others

– on a man – to help her and her child. In *Mother, Madonna, Whore*, the psychoanalyst Estela Welldon has produced a disturbing account of the connections between violence against children and our prevailing concept of motherhood: 'Our whole culture supports the idea that mothers have complete dominion over their babies; thus we encourage the very ideas the perverse mother exploits.' She continues, 'perhaps if women had a longer tradition of belonging to the power structure their attitudes to men and children would not be governed, as they are now, by a weakness they strive to turn into possessiveness and control.' The woman who shocks us because she does not notice that her husband is sleeping with their daughter; or who stands by and lets it happen; or helps to organise a photography session or prostitution with her child or children, bears on her the marks of her own upbringing and her own mother's dominion; but she's also integrated into current, social deterioration, and the politics of the family.

A significant number of men in families where children are neglected, beaten, tortured, and 'fail to thrive' are not their fathers, but their stepfathers, or their mother's boyfriend. It's common to react by bitterly blaming the woman for allowing such a man near her and her children and failing to defend them, like a tigress, like a she-bear, with that famous maternal instinct that is so poorly understood, so little fostered, and so completely unrewarded. Finding a lover is one of the means of escape built into the system of childcare as it is presently organised for women; even though many of these temporary stepfathers don't hand over much money, it seems. A consequence of the privatisation of the child can be the prostitution of the mother, not professionally, but experientially, because the expectations of society, reflected in the social benefit structure just as in pulp romances, lean towards the solution of finding the right man with the right car, like the knight on the charger in the last page.

Child abuse, as battery and as rape or other forms of sexual assault, presents us with an image of our worst selves, an extreme picture of brutality. But it is a brutality we must also recognise, in the midst of crying out against it, as contiguous with the widespread brutalisation which children witness and suffer, alongside and with the grown-ups who live with them. When the tabloids bay for the blood of doctors and social workers who have discovered child abuse – they too are conjuring a preserve of innocence – the family – where such things must never happen, and they are repudiating the part they play in the making of the world that has forfeited the innocence they claim to cherish. They are also the first to call down vengeance on child molesters and rapists, as if they knew nothing of the pleasure of violence, the commitment to sensational gratification, or the religion of forbidden sexual experiment.

The Pushchair

Few families use prams any more; the pushchair on the other hand is adapted for urban life. Lightweight, folded with a quick jerk of the wrist and a single kick of the foot, it comes complete with bottom tray for shopping (and ballast), attachable pannier at the back, and, in case of rain, an all-over clear plastic canopy so that the child inside can take in the view and keep dry at the same time. When pushchairs came in, they revolutionised the life of urban mothers.

Have you seen a woman going to the West End with her children? Say she is going to Oxford Street to buy her five-year-old the uniform and jumper she needs for starting school. Such things are cheaper in the big department stores. It is raining, the new baby is in the pushchair, under the PVC baldaquin. When they reach the Tube station, the baby is dry, and sedated from his bumpy and airless passage. The five-year-old is fine in gumboots and mac; Mum, like a rickshaw driver, with no spare hand for an umbrella, has been exposed to the elements. At the top of the escalators, she unzips the plastic canopy and lifts the baby out – it's recommended 'for safety's sake' to fold pushchairs in the Underground. The baby is cross at the sharp contrast, the sudden interruption to his sleep. She kicks the pushchair shut, and gives it to the little girl to carry down to the platform (at this stage she hasn't yet done any shopping, so the vehicle is still neat and light). Then she sees that the escalator isn't working.

There's a printed notice in which London Transport apologises for the repairs, which 'will be completed as soon as possible'. No one is in sight. No hammerings rise from below. 'I don't believe you', someone has written.

As her elder child negotiates the narrow twist of the emergency stairs, slowly, slowly, her hand on the filthy rail, minding she doesn't sniff too hard the odd stains and or tread in this and that, the mother waits for her, and the baby gets heavier and heavier on her arm . . .

So we leave them, remembering that by the time Mum has bought the uniform, she will have done this four times at least, if she doesn't have to change lines.

And about the pushchair, some paediatricians now think they aren't very good, because their small wheels jar the undeveloped spine. It was really designed to make it possible for mothers and children to do things together and was inspired by the thinking that the nurture of the early years shaped the future for the better, that separation could blight the personality in bud. Like many advances in modern childcare, the pushchair helps to bond mother and child.

Little monsters

MOTHERHOOD is its own reward. Oh yes? When you are reproached for leaving your child alone when you go to work, or blamed if you don't find a job; no wonder women hit their children in the street; no wonder the bawling child, pinioned in the supermarket cart and red with fury at the sight of the glittering sweet counter, is silenced by a blow and stoppered with a lump of boiled sugar or a stick of chocolate or a dummy that moments before was on the filthy floor. It was the reason I wanted to write this pamphlet, that mothers in the streets round me behaved so angrily with their children.

Economic stress magnifies the perception of kids as monsters, and this perception in turn works to justify the bitter, furious punitiveness of relations between parent and child. You must have heard the screaming children, who scream all the more when their raging mother jerks their arm or shouts at them: the 'discipline' provokes more grief, it only serves to remind all around that the task of mothering is tough, the little blighters are abominable, the job is thankless. Hitting children winds everyone – parent, infant, passers-by – into a knot of ever tightening stress. The proximity caused by lack of space, lack of work, lack of minders, lack of time intensifies the deeply felt helplessness of adults facing baby power, child demands. The innocent becomes menacing, the hapless malignant.

Popular mythology strengthens the current attitude, and significantly, far beyond the circles of the disadvantaged and the poor, the single mother or the divorcee. The cost of children, in energy, time, emotion as well as money, takes its toll. In films, in television drama produced by people who haven't ever whacked a child in a public place in sheer desperation, kids have been regularly represented as actually possessed by the devil (*Rosemary's Baby*, *The Exorcist*) and the preternatural strength of babies, in no way emanating from their progenitors, but appearing out of the blue to overwhelm them utterly, has become a recurrent theme of recent fiction. Writers as different as Anita Brookner (in *Latecomers*), Victoria Glendinning (in *The Grown-ups*), Marianne Wiggins (*John Dollar*) and Martin Amis in *London Fields* have introduced overpowering infants, the inheritors of romantic vitalism, possessed by splendid generous unconsciousness of might. Wicked children used to be old enough, but not quite old enough to know better, as in *The Turn of the Screw* or *High Wind in Jamaica* or *Lord of the Flies*. But now, it is babies who are monstrous, knowing, not innocent, devouring, not vulnerable. Among this literary throng of malignant cherubim, bursting with flesh, vociferating desire, the cartoonist Heath has created a memorable character, Baby, who looms so large in his parents' lives that he literally bursts out of their home, and when he needs new clothes, the balloons read: (Mother): 'I went to buy him a new outfit today . . . They're sending me an estimate.'

42

Baby bawling in bed between them bears the caption, 'We mustn't let him get between us.' The dark humour faces up to childpower: the appearance of the tyrannical toddler in caricature is the equivalent of mother-in-law jokes, coping with unwelcome, half-tolerated authority, voicing rebellion so as not to look like too much of a doormat. (There's a grudging affection in the jibes, too, of course, as there is in the pet names, 'pest' and 'nuisance' and 'little horror' and 'menace'. When a mother says, 'Come on, trouble,' to her three-year-old in a shop, she can mean it kindly.)

The monster baby represents the flip side of a new awareness of children's rights and presence; they haven't been increasing to an undivided reception. The black humour perceives power in powerlessness because a small amount of recognition of the child's independence has been realised recently, and needs have been recognised. It also reflects the increasing separation between the spheres of experience: in this sense, as well, children are coming to occupy the place of women, the mysterious, unknowable, compelling site of otherness, filled with power, yet unable to exercise it altogether, and all the more threatening for that, inviting abuse though innocent, culpable without cause – the analogy with female sexuality becomes irrepressible.

Mother

In a corner of the Post Office, a baby is wailing. It's not an infant, because it's using words. It's by the letter boxes, beyond the straggling lines to the counters, strapped in. The Post Office is crowded, there are about eight lines shuffling forward to different clerks. The child's plastic canopy is folded back, and it's straining against the belt, trying to get out.

'Mummy!' it cries. 'Mummy, help me!' When the cry comes again, some people in line begin to twitch; we look about, looking for the mother. No one is forthcoming, no one identifiable.

My turn comes. I ask for twenty second-class stamps.

'Mummeeee! Help me!' The wail again. It has that edge to the ends of the words that cut you like a blade; I feel them, flush against my skin. I'm not the only one, the cry passes through the queue, it is making all of us jumpy.

I want to go over to the baby, but I'm not the mother, and I'll only make things worse, she might be furious with an interfering stranger who has apparently set her child off in a paroxysm of fright.

At this moment, an older child, about five, goes up, pats the squaller's shoulder and points. We follow the older child's finger. Now we know who the mother is.

She's at the furthest counter. She turns, leans out, focuses on the pair of kids at the other end of the hall. Raven-haired, composed, rather glamorous. She calls out,

'Lee, what have you done to him now? Leave him alone!'

The child pushes up with his feet on the bar of the pushchair, but the straps hold him back. Now he's seen her, he bawls louder.

44

'Mummee! Mumm-eee! Help me!'

In the next line to mine, an old man, in a beard, mutters 'Why not bring him over to you, so he's near you.'

The woman ahead of him, young, in purple leopard leggings and a sticky up haircut, shakes her head and tells the clerk,

'You give in to their squawking once and they'll be on at you forever – I know, I got three.'

'That's not true,' I find myself saying.

'How many children you got then? They must be real spoiled brats.'

'One,' I snap back, 'and he's not.'

She ignores this, she turns back to the glass, and says, loudly enough so we can all hear,

'Why's it always all down to the mothers anyway?'

Little angels

THE MONSTER child reflects uneasiness about the beast in all of us; but it coexists with another sacred infant, who holds up a mirror to human possibility at the opposite pole: for every demon child in this world, there's a cherub who belongs in everyone's lost childhood – the paradise where everything, even sex, was innocent.

The newborn Christ symbolised love, the redeeming love of God for humanity, and the cult of the Child Jesus flourishes in Catholic countries like Italy and Spain where children move among adults in public and in private in an atmosphere of tolerance and affection. Although Augustinian doctrine defined the newborn child as the habitation of the Devil, popular language – verbal and visual – paid little attention. Babies symbolise innocence, and those who do them harm are so many Herods. A few Puritans waxed menacingly about instincts of darkness in the untutored soul, and methods of discipline and education of horrendous cruelty were developed, both in England and New England. But someone like John Earle, Bishop of Salisbury could write, in 1628: 'A Child is . . . a man in a small letter, yet the best copy of Adam before he tasted of Eve or the apple.'

Freud upset his colleagues when he defined, in the language of scientific objectivity, something mothers and nursemaids had always known, the 'polymorphous perversity' of infants; his findings connect with the mystique of the female child in particular – the *femme enfant* idolised by the surrealists, who believed that infantile sexuality endows the young with the thrilling power of unashamed, uninhibited knowledge. The lessons of nineteenth century exploration and of pioneer anthropology also expanded the view of children's precocity and capacity: in Kipling, Mowgli is in revolt against human society, and Kim too lives as a loner in the society that employs him for his skills and cunning; Malinowski and Margaret Mead revealed the possibilities of a discrete social group, the Pacific islanders' 'republic of children', who enjoyed self-reliance, playfulness in sexual experiments, an idyllic lack of restraint or penalties, and above all, freedom from consequences of their transgressions against the Western code of childhood innocence.

The closeness of children to an ideal humanity is presumed in many responses to their conditions or treatment: besides the assault on the child's body and the perversion of parental power, the sexual violation of children excites outrage because immaterial innocence has also been exploited and destroyed. The desire for that innocence to remain inviolate isn't only altruistic, it isn't only for the children's sake that we want their vulnerability respected and kept safe. It is for our own sakes too, to help us entertain a vision of the possibilities for good. This isn't meant by way of criticism of the horror and alarm over the incidence of crimes against children, but rather, as clarification. Again, rather like the damsel in distress who transforms a wandering adventurer into a knight errant and proves his chivalry, the fragile, undefended and innocent child provides a lonely chance of showing disinterestedness in a world where the weak go to the wall. The philosophy of love, something the Greeks and the Christian Neo-Platonists were eager to discuss, pursuing an elusive understanding of what this highest good might mean, has dropped from contemporary discourse, and the hard questions, about the varieties of love and the ways society can help or hinder their expression, have not been faced, because romantic ideas about instinct and nature are clamouring for attention, and the love of children is assumed.

Children don't appear very much in the mass media, except for reports of massacres, natural disasters, or acts of violence closer to home, where their presence indicates the degree of the catastrophe. They're used in adverts, however, to guarantee purity and promise – of the product, the life insurance policy, the airline, the investment company, in the same way that 'nature' – cascading waters, green glades in the background – makes any strong alcohol appear healthy as spring. Volkswagen published a photograph of a bare-chested man and baby with the message: 'Six months free unleaded petrol for all new deliveries', neatly identifying themselves with green consciences and child-friendliness, and humanising the invisible Golf or Jetta in the form of a naked baby.

Children also enter the imagery of power: the fact of having children is immensely important to self-esteem and a good public image. When politicians or magnates are interviewed, they surround themselves with their offspring. Mrs Thatcher chose to celebrate the tenth anniversary of her reign with a photo opportunity featuring her first grandchild, flown in for the occasion. Wives, or husbands, no longer appear by the subject's side – this now seems somehow demeaning to the spouse and somehow sentimental – unless their child or children are present. Most frequently of all, fathers will pose with children on their own. To hoist a son on one's shoulders shows one has the right values, that one is a person with priorities, a disinterested man who cannot be accused of thinking only of the recompenses accruing to his labour, or of never giving anything away for free. ('The powers of a parent are not bestowed . . . as a recompense.') The performance of fatherhood can be definitely disinfectant of power. A child is a warranty of selflessness, considered innate in a mother, not learned, and therefore less significantly virtuous than in a father. Yet when the same fathers of these highly visible toddlers are travelling, they will find that the facilities to change nappies are only in the Ladies.

The Teddy Bear

The soft toy is new, it was only invented at the end of the last century, and even then it wasn't very soft, not like the bears and other creatures that fill almost a whole floor of Hamley's. Children in the portraits of seventeenth century aristocrats sometimes hold dolls, stiffly swaddled around a wooden body, but then and later the animals depicted are usually real: lambs, dogs, goats, cats, and birds, themselves often babies of their kind, were the first playthings.

The teddy bear was named after President Teddy Roosevelt, who was a keen hunter, especially of grizzlies, symbol of native America. In 1902 he refused to shoot a bear cub after killing its mother, and the new toy was nicknamed after his act of mercy. Since then, manufacturers have created Mummy bears in aprons and Daddy bears in jeans, there have been Pooh and Paddington and Aloysius, and soft toys have taken the shape of every furry species on the planet and many more even less cuddly in their natural state than a grizzly bear: killer whales, snails, spiders and snakes.

The transitional object was defined by D. W. Winnicott in the fifties: now, in Hamley's, grown-ups sigh and cry out with pleasure alongside their children. Grannies and teenagers count out funds for a furry hedgehog, a baby deer, a lion cub, stretching themselves to acquire the latest kind from Germany, the very softest and fluffiest and most cuddly animals of all (at around thirty pounds each).

A corpulent businessman on his own is sampling different animals, now plunging his face into the plush of a squirrel, now petting the silky face of a kitten, or palpating the deep pelt of a sweet brown owl. He is smiling to himself, with deep unselfconscious happiness, while all around hands dive in the soft heaps of toys, and voices cry out, 'Feel this one, oh, oh, oh, isn't he gorgeous?'

It is when we put away childish things, that we lose charity. Or so it now seems to us. The department of soft toys is a giant therapy cell, a kind of Woody Allen dream of padded bliss and infantile regression, where the sense of touch – which must be kept in its place so strictly after childhood – can be given free rein, and allowed to stimulate a sweet, a *touching* return to tenderness and comfort, in the same way as a child can restore hope in the existence of love. The soft toy may be like a votive candle, offered to children by us penitents, so that they will intercede on our behalf and give access to that place of pleasure children still inhabit; or so the one who prays believes, imputing to the child many things children cannot know, nor promise to be.

Consuming children

AS CHILDREN become more and more costly – to the rich who want to give them sleep-over all-night video parties and holidays abroad and private schools and their own room and or even their own floor in the house, to the poor who need a place to live in the first place and work to pay for it – they become hedged by divinity, a treasure, a focus, a guarantee of the elusive, the immaterial significance of life. And because childhood now partakes of the sacred, because it has become a blissful never-never land you don't ever want to leave, people who can afford expensive children can also afford to preserve their childhood longer, by employing childcare that keeps them under surveillance, 'off the street', by buying them extended years in education, by furnishing them a room of their own, which can help keep them at home. The more 'emotionally priceless', the more 'economically useless' children become.

The paradox sheds some light on the condition of childhood: children are still not to be seen or heard, in spite of the recent efforts of the law, if it can be arranged. The more money a family has, the more the children are segregated. In a reader's survey in the magazine *Harpers & Queen*, the mothers who responded agreed that children should have their own TV set in their own quarters, that earphones were one of the best inventions ever and very useful on car journeys to the country at weekends. It hardly needs pointing out that the most expensive schools in the country are for full-time boarders, that the richest families spend the most money to send their children away for the longest periods of education – seven to nineteen – of any country in the world.

The market force child is subject to the conditions of another valuable commodity in the contemporary world, the art object: the more priceless the work, the more conservation it needs, the more distance is placed between it and the public, the more humidity and temperature controls are applied, so that it will last long (forever) and not be harmed; the less valuable the work, the more it can travel, be exposed to scrutiny, passed from hand to hand. The analogies with the child today don't have to be pressed: one mother in the *Harpers* survey remarked openly, 'there are expensive children and cheap children, just as there are expensive women and cheap women.'

The market's dream is to make every child expensive; children have become a consumer target, through their parents' pockets, and their guilt. You can buy kids' prêt-à-porter from Kenzo or Sonia Rykiel; beauty products for babies – perfumes and cosmetics far more expensive and exotic than zinc ointment – have been devised for 'Yuppie Puppies'.

When today's producers force the children's market to expand, they are continuing a process which began only in the last century, with the mass manufacturing of toys and the first large scale publishing of books aimed exclusively at children. Children's literature began by appealing to broad age-bands; now books are produced, like clothes, with age specifications on the jacket – for nine-year-olds, for eleven-year-olds. The first children's encyclopaedia appeared only in 1910; educational publishing for homes as well as for schools is now an important British export. Museums and galleries have introduced workshops, quizzes, lecture series for children of all ages; there has never been anything to compare in history before with the modern toyshop.

These are advances. But the government's squeeze on public subsidies has forced free institutions to charge, though they do their best with family and school concessions. The main drawback is that the child is cast as a consumer, who can dig deep into adult pockets: the toy industry in Britain is worth £900 million a year, and an average of £80 was spent on every child at Christmas 1987.

Television programmes that consist of a single half hour commercial – for GI Joe or He Man or Masters of the Universe – are known to children as 'toy-toons'. They will flourish when television is opened to competition according to the principles of deregulation (a word which makes its entrance into the OED this year).

Less choice in the type and quality of kids' programmes will result from market forces' play in TV. With toys, and books, where competition has led to greater quality as well as enormously geared-up quantities, the range of choice doesn't trail a corresponding variety of consumer. As Ralf Dahrendorf has strikingly pointed out, 'Greater choice does not

54

lead to greater access.' If money is not spent maintaining school libraries, all the brilliant and careful writing for children of all ages will not circulate as it should. The issue is not how full the toy departments are with bright, clever, enhancing games, but who enjoys title to enjoy them.

Thatcher's families

'Truly it is not easy to bring up a family.'

King Babar

DO CHILDREN grow up too soon? Or are we only asking them to stay young to preserve an illusion for us of a better world? The separation of the states of adulthood and childhood is vital to the maintenance of the innocence about which we care: yet again, the market force child cannot be kept apart unless huge investments are made – in the case of children, in their education, in housing, in outdoor space, in entertainment, and television, the electronic baby-minder for all those out of school hours.

Child abuse is the crime our decade has diagnosed because a crisis exists, beyond the immediate victims and their assailants, suspected or otherwise, about the decay of goodness; when a child a week is dying as a consequence of family violence, we are looking at a reality that magnifies all doubts about human nature. Children are like the planet, they bear the imprint of our deeds, they embody our hopes – and our transgressions. It isn't a coincidence that the enrolment in Green groups of one kind and another is growing apace, that obsessive – and probably justified – anxiety about polluted food and water has dominated recent politics; the search is on to find something –

and someone – uncontaminated and preserve their innocence. Children could be in this respect the repository of adult fantasies and illusions; it is possible we have it all wrong, and they would prefer to grow up at thirteen, leave school, work, smoke, marry and so forth, and they know better (and some child psychologists agree). It is possible that the desire to preserve an ideal of innocence, of learning, of unharmed apprenticeship to living, of love, is another arbitrary imposition grown-ups make upon children. But I for one believe in children's rights to their childhood, and childhood means freedom from pain, from coercion, from violence, the enjoyment of confidence and security and safety, access to food, shelter, and the development of skills.

Much has been done over the last ten years to make life hard for parents – and for parents, read above all, mothers. And everything that makes life hard for parents makes it harder for children. In the era of the market force child, children are suffering, and with them, all of us are being damaged. The privatised baby does not belong in the fantasy family of Fifties suburbia, for which some of the present government thinking seems to yearn, because, in the account book of the dying welfare state, the columns won't balance. When your mother is at work, her situation will not be eased: she will hunt for adequate care that she can afford and anxiety will gnaw her that she has not found it. You, her children, will suffer, and she will suffer for you and because of you, which will add to your sum of suffering. The low consideration of motherhood clashes with the ascribed value of children: the job of

57

childcare, by parents and others, must be given its due.

The reality of children collides with their idealisation in more abstract ways too: children are loved for not being like adults, and when they begin to develop, with human failings as well as strengths, they are blamed for falling short of the ideal of child-likeness. In the words of Adam Smith, 'The qualities needed to advance are in children the reprehensible ones.' Children cannot be expected to be better than people; to be different from the people among whom they live.

Given the problems parents and children face, given the failure to thrive the decade has overseen, the simple response would be to stop making families altogether. Maybe however, as children aren't actually dying out, self-interest isn't the over-riding motive of human conduct. It's a wonder – perhaps even a remaining trace of a deep, buried capacity for love – that people continue to have them at all.

About the Author

MARINA WARNER is a distinguished writer and critic. Her books include: *Alone of All Her Sex: the myth and cult of the Virgin Mary* and *Monuments and Maidens: the allegory of the female form*. She has also written children's books and novels. Her third novel, *The Lost Father*, was published last year.

CHATTO
CounterBlasts

Also available in bookshops now:-

Forthcoming Chatto CounterBlasts

CounterBlasts to be published in 1990 include:-

plus pamphlets from Michael Holroyd, Hanif Kureishi, Michael Ignatieff, Edward Mortimer and Susannah Clapp

If you want to join in the debate, and if you want to know more about **CounterBlasts**, the writers and the issues, then write to:

Random House UK Ltd, Freepost 5066, Dept MH, London WC1B 3BR